Editor  April McCroskie
Language Consultant  Prof Viv Edwards
Natural History Consultant  Dr Gerald Legg

**David Stewart** has written many non-fiction books for children. He lives in Brighton with his wife and young son.

**Carolyn Scrace** is a graduate of Brighton College of Art, specialising in design and illustration. She has worked in animation, advertising and children's fiction. She is a major contributor to the popular *Worldwise* series.

**Professor Viv Edwards** is professor of Language in Education and director of the *Reading and Language Information Centre* at the University of Reading.

**Dr Gerald Legg** holds a doctorate in zoology from Manchester University. His current position is biologist at the Booth Museum of Natural History in Brighton.

**David Salariya** was born in Dundee, Scotland, where he studied illustration and printmaking, concentrating on book design in his postgraduate year. He has designed and created many new series of children's books for publishers in the U.K. and overseas.

An SBC Book conceived, edited and designed by
The Salariya Book Company
25 Marlborough Place Brighton BN1 1UB

©The Salariya Book Company Ltd MCMXCVII

A CIP catalogue record for this book is available from the British Library

ISBN 0 7496 2653 4 (hbk)
ISBN 0 7496 3143 0 (pbk)
Dewey Classification 597.8

First published in Great Britain in 1997
Franklin Watts
96 Leonard Street
London EC2A 4XD

Franklin Watts Australia
14 Mars Road
Lane Cove
NSW 2066

Printed in Belgium

# lifecycles

# From Tadpole to Frog

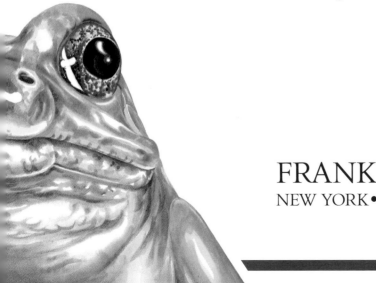

Written by David Stewart
Illustrated by Carolyn Scrace

Created & Designed by David Salariya

W
FRANKLIN WATTS
NEW YORK • LONDON • SYDNEY

A frog begins life as an egg. A tadpole hatches from the egg. The tadpole grows into a froglet, and finally into a frog. In this book you can see this amazing life cycle unfold.

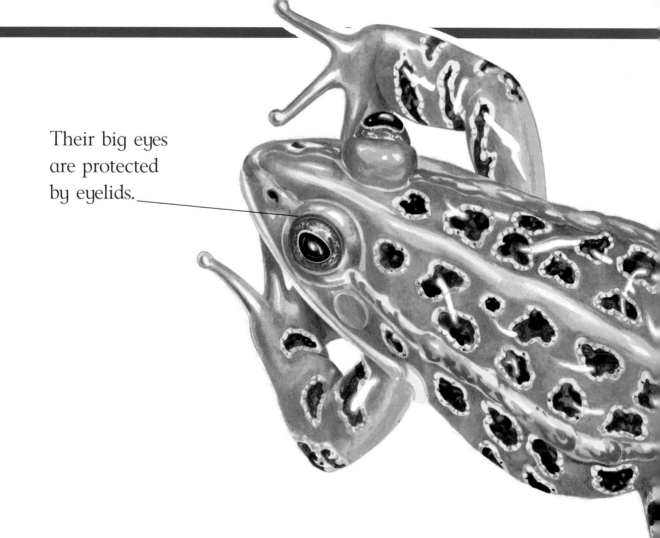

Their big eyes
are protected
by eyelids.

Frogs live most of the time
in or near water. Their strong
back legs, with webbed feet,
are good for swimming.

Frogs can live
in water and
on land.
Animals that
can do this are
called amphibians.

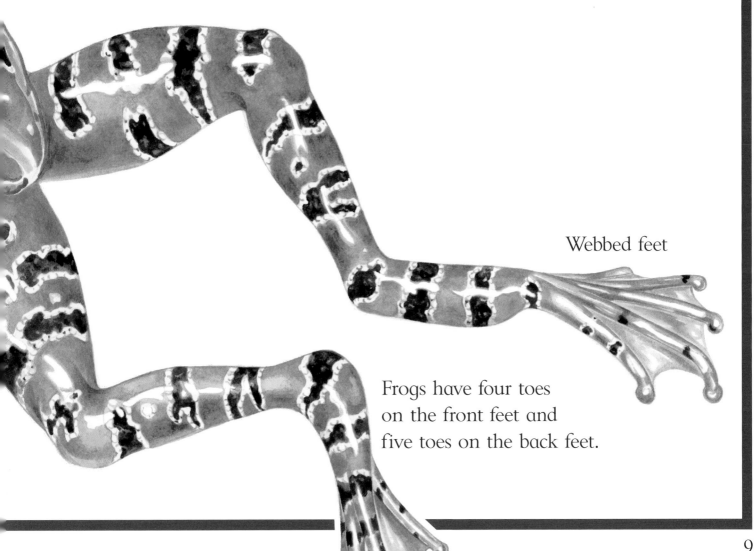

Webbed feet

Frogs have four toes
on the front feet and
five toes on the back feet.

In spring the female frog lays eggs,
and the male frog covers them
with a liquid called sperm.
The eggs are fertilized
by the sperm and
begin to grow.

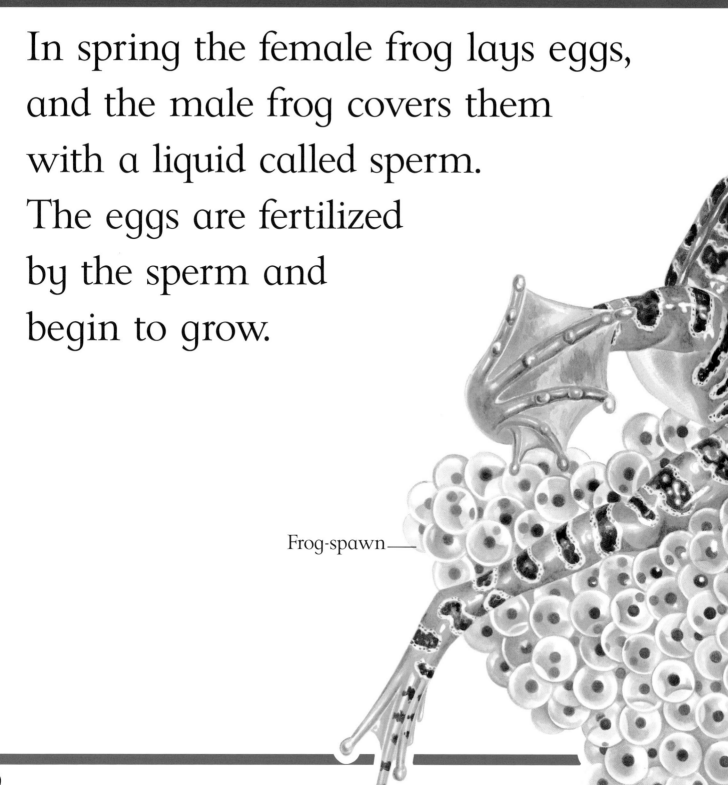

Frog-spawn——

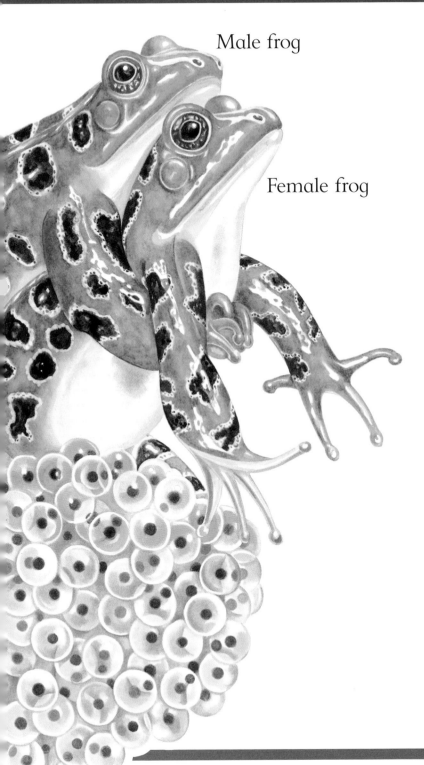

Male frog

Female frog

The eggs stick
together to form
frog-spawn.
The frog-spawn
floats to the top
of the water.

# Each egg grows inside a ball of jelly.

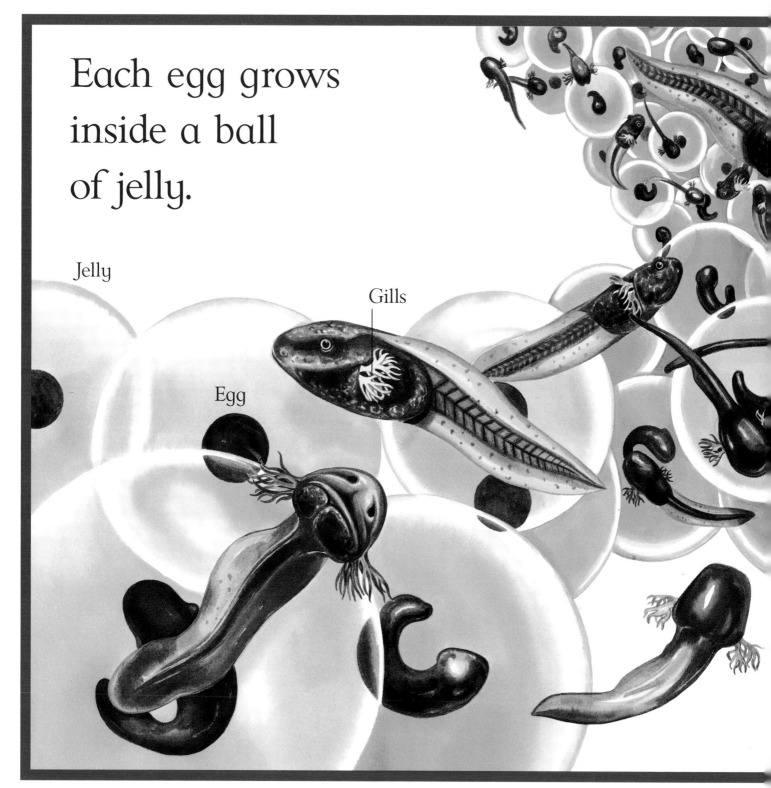

Jelly

Gills

Egg

Tadpole

A few days later
the tadpoles hatch out.
They live under water
and breathe through
their gills.

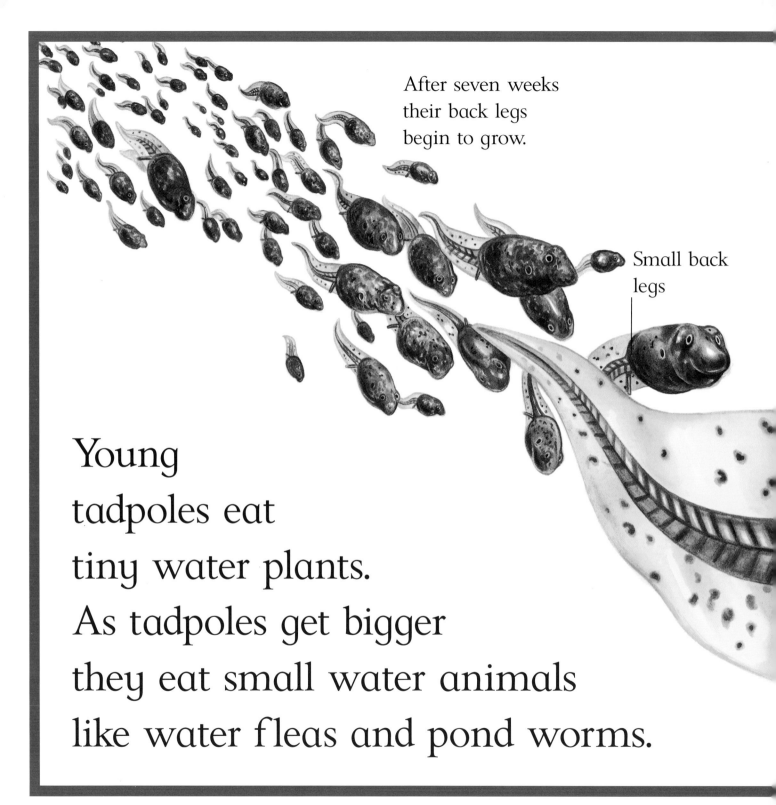

After seven weeks
their back legs
begin to grow.

Small back
legs

Young
tadpoles eat
tiny water plants.
As tadpoles get bigger
they eat small water animals
like water fleas and pond worms.

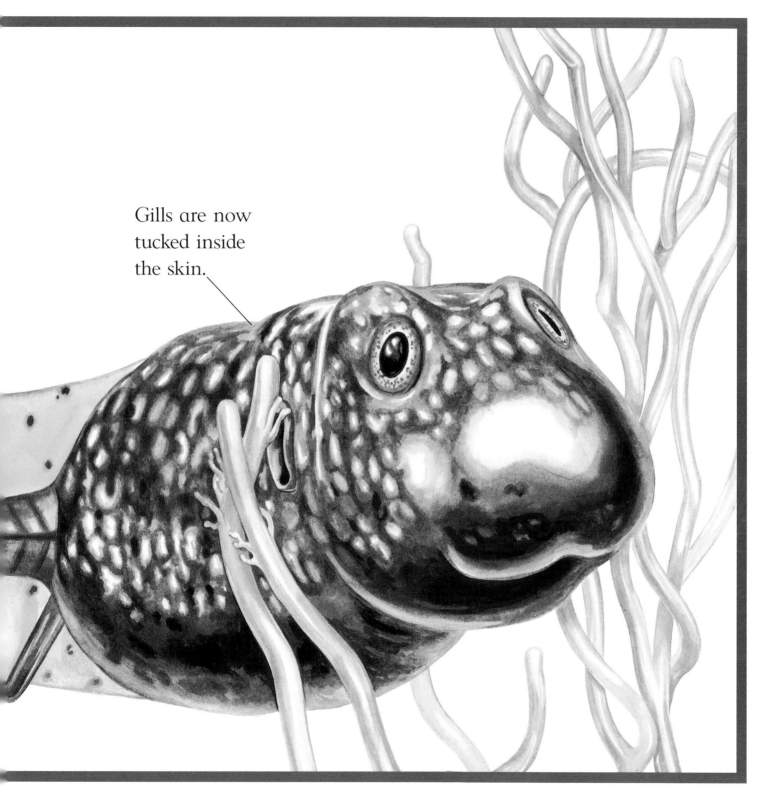

Gills are now
tucked inside
the skin.

The tail shrinks.
After nine weeks
front legs grow
near where the gills
used to be.

Before, the tadpoles used
their gills to breathe.
Now they use
their lungs.

After twelve weeks
the tadpoles can
swim to the surface
of the water and
breathe in air.

Only the back legs
are used for
swimming.

Webbed toes help
the young frog
to swim faster.

After three months
the tadpoles have
become young frogs,
and are called froglets.
Frogs are amphibians.
This means that
they can live
in or out of water.
They have long,
sticky tongues that are
good for catching insects.

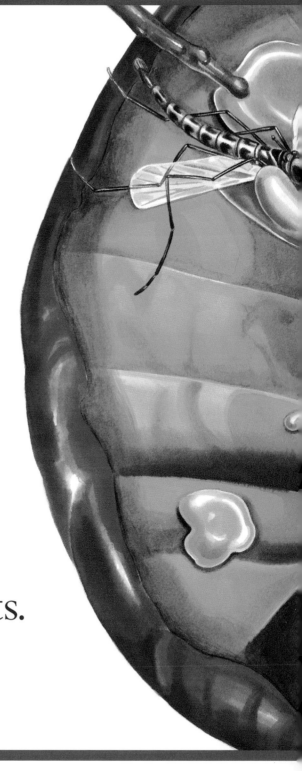

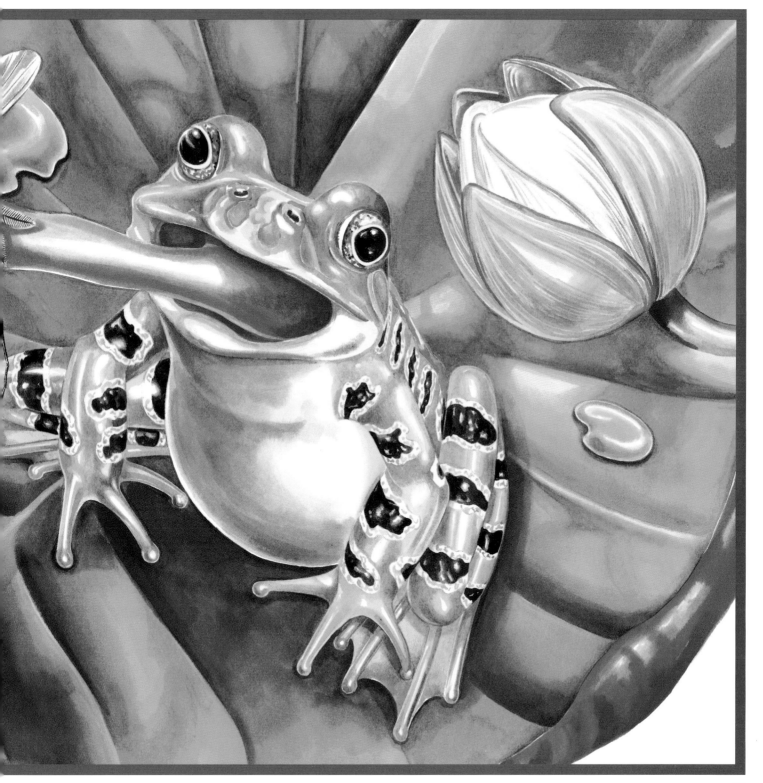

Froglets face many dangers.
Some animals like to catch
and eat them.

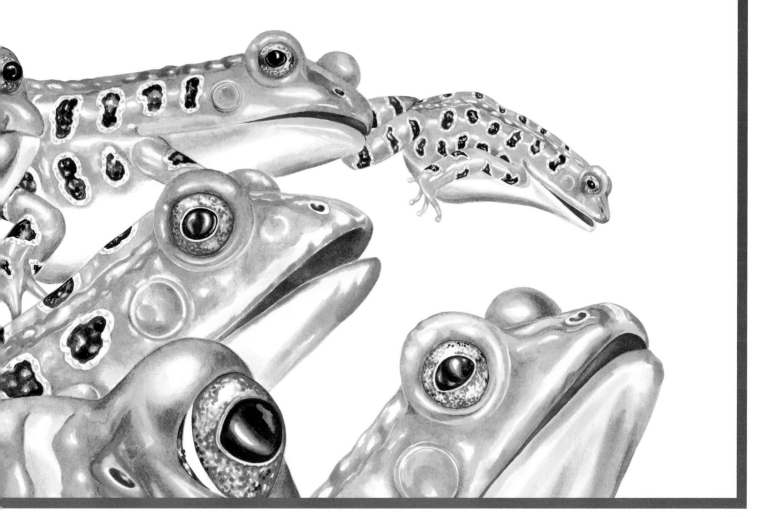

Frogs grow up to look like their parents.
When she is three years old,
the female frog will lay eggs.

Vocal sac

Male frog

Vocal sac

The male frog
tries to attract
the female.

Female frog

He expands his vocal sacs
and sings to her.

# Frog facts

A frog is an amphibian. Amphibians begin their lives in water.

The smallest amphibian is an arrow poison frog from Cuba. It is about one centimetre long.

Frogs are cold-blooded creatures. Their body temperature changes with the temperature around them.

Frogs have smooth, wet skin. Toads have dry, bumpy skin.

Some frogs live in trees. There are over 300 species of tree frog.

Tree frogs have large webbed feet. This helps them leap between trees.

A species of frog called the White's tree frog has disc-shaped toes that act like suckers. These help it to cling to branches.

Tree frogs live on insects and on the water that collects in leaves.

**The growth of a frog**

In the pictures below you can see the way a frog grows. First, the frog's egg hatches into a tadpole. Next, a tadpole becomes a young froglet. Finally, a froglet grows into a frog.

| Egg | 1 week | 7 weeks | 9 weeks | 12 weeks | 14 weeks |

In the tropical forests of Asia, the flying frog can "fly" for about 14 metres. It has big webbed feet that act like birds' wings.

A rare frog from New Zealand lives far from water. It does not have tadpoles. Small frogs emerge straight from the eggs.

Arrow poison frogs are found in Central and South America. They produce the most lethal poisons of any creature.

The largest frog is the goliath frog of western Africa. It can grow to a length of about one metre and weighs over three kilograms.

20 weeks

Fully grown

# Frog words

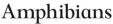

**Amphibians**
Creatures able to live in water or on land. They begin their lives in water.

**Expand**
Make bigger.

**Froglet**
A young frog.

**Fertilization**
When an egg and sperm join together. The egg and sperm will become a baby.

**Frog-spawn**
The sticky eggs that float on the surface of the water. Tadpoles hatch from frog-spawn.

**Gills**
These are needed by creatures to breathe under water. They are outside the body.

**Lungs**
These are needed by creatures to breathe air. They are inside the body.

**Species**
A group of animals that look alike, live in the same way and produce young that do the same.

**Sperm**
The liquid from the male that joins the egg from the female to produce a baby.

**Tadpole**
The small creature that hatches from a frog's egg.

**Vocal sac**
The part of a frog's throat that allows it to make a croaking sound.

**Webbed feet**
Feet with stretched skin between the toes. Webbed feet help frogs to swim.

# Index

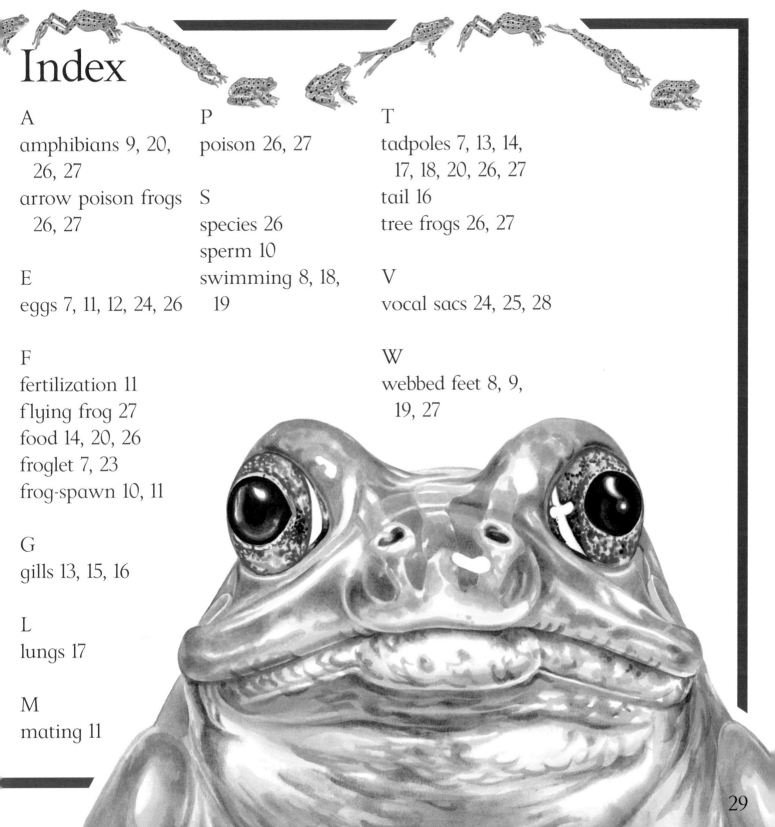